Original title:
The Lace Beneath the Clouds



Author: Clara Whitfield
ISBN HARDBACK: 978-1-80586-024-2
ISBN PAPERBACK: 978-1-80586-496-7

## Chasing Celestial Stitches

In the sky, a tangled thread,
Clouds are dancing, 'round they spread.
One made of fluff, one jumpy glee,
Stitching joy for all to see.

A kite caught high, like a fish on a line,
Yanking on dreams with a giggle so fine.
Twisting and turning, oh, what a sight,
Chasing the sun, it’s a comical flight.

## Patterns in the Skyline

Look at the clouds, oh what a game,
They're draping patterns, yet none are the same.
A floating taco, a castle of pie,
What's next in this sky? A dancing french fry?

The sun peeks out, and clouds take a bow,
Making faces, as if to say, 'Wow!'
A patchwork quilt, stitched by the breeze,
Puffs of laughter that tickle the trees.

## A Tangle of Air and Light

The wind weaves ribbons from stars so bright,
Tickling the heavens with pure delight.
A flurry of giggles, a shimmer of rays,
Unruly and wondrous, in funny displays.

Silly confetti, we toss to the sky,
Where rainbows twist, and the puffy clouds sigh.
Laughter takes wing on a zephyr's soft flow,
As we chase after dreams, like kids in the snow.

## Veils of Ethereal Grace

A whimsical waltz, soft and absurd,
Clouds wear their veils, not a heavy word.
Giggling fairies in a cottony sea,
Mastering dance with the utmost glee.

A tiptoe ballet on a sunbeam so bright,
Where clouds and giggles unite for a night.
Winds whisper secrets, just silly and light,
Under the moon, they give us a fright!

## Golden Threads Across the Horizon

Golden strands stretch wide and bright,
Woven whispers dance in flight.
Bumbling bees in fancy dress,
Buzzing jokes, oh what a mess!

Kites flying high, a tug-of-war,
Chasing tails, they aim for more.
Laughter floats like dandelion seeds,
Spreading joy, fulfilling needs.

## Skies Drenched in Silken Traces

In the sky, a painter’s cheer,
Brush strokes wild, nothing to fear.
Cotton candy clouds do tease,
Can’t catch them, oh, what a breeze!

Silly hats on each puffed face,
Wobble, giggle, what a race!
Each sunbeam throws a quirky shade,
Help! I’m lost in this parade!

## The Ethereal Dance of Sunlight

Sunlight waltzes, full of glee,
Twirls with shadows, oh so free.
Glimmers teasing, here and there,
They play tag in the open air.

A cheeky squirrel drops a nut,
While sunlight sings, 'Just let it strut!'
Bouncing beams and giggling rays,
Chasing down the cloudy maze.

## Clouds Intertwined with Dreams

Fluffy giants drift and sway,
Plotting mischief in the gray.
Knitting wishes, soft and grand,
Spinning thoughts like grains of sand.

Behind the curtain, a giggle's heard,
As dreams dare to speak a word.
Floating high on whimsy's trail,
Come along, let's laugh and sail!

## Threads of Solitude Above

In the sky, a threadbare joke,
Clouds wear gowns made of hope.
Laughter drips like melting ice,
Whimsical whims, oh so nice!

Patchwork dreams drift without care,
Floating hats and socks in air.
A squirrel winks at a wooly sheep,
As breezes carry secrets deep.

Twisted taffy twists in grace,
Tickled winds begin to race.
Up there, even frowns can swish,
Puffy puns make fluffy wishes!

So let's knit in colors bold,
With laughter that never gets old.
Flying high on threads of cheer,
Stitching giggles, year by year.

## Weaving Echoes in the Twilight

Twilight weaves with golden thread,
A kitten snorts, then turns to bed.
Voices echo, loud and bright,
Dancing shadows in the night.

Pigeons in hats strut and prance,
While moonlight gives the stars a chance.
Whispered secrets, laughing loud,
Underneath the dreamy shroud.

Knitted giggles tie the night,
As frogs in tuxes leap in flight.
Every echo tells a tale,
Of creatures plotting, never pale.

So let's toast to midnight fun,
With puns and beats to make us run.
The twilight sky, a grand ballet,
Where laughter lives and dreams will play.

## Shadows of Color Amongst the Clouds

Colors burst from silent hush,
While rubber ducks begin to blush.
Underneath a fluffy hat,
A rainbow grazes a feisty cat.

Crayons dance on cotton fluff,
Making mischief, oh so tough.
A poodle prances, tail held high,
Painting dreams in the sky.

With giggles sewn in every seam,
The clouds conspire in a dream.
Socks and shoes all mixed design,
A soft parade, so divine!

So here we laugh and play around,
With skybound jokes that know no bound.
The colors swirl, the shadows cheer,
In this circus atmosphere!

## Dreams Draped in Serenity

In the sky where two socks meet,
Clouds gather for a big ol' feast.
They serve up dreams like grilled cheese,
Fluffy pancakes on a breeze.

Underneath, the world's a stage,
Where rubber chickens steal the rage.
Dancing rainbows paint a grin,
While puddles play tag with the wind.

## Ethereal Ties and Time

Time tickles with its feather duster,
As clouds wear hats, oh so cluster.
A ticklish breeze blows 'round the bend,
Where giggles linger just like trends.

Here balloons become the stars of night,
And every comet’s a plastic kite.
Laughter floats on cotton candy,
With silly thoughts that taste like brandy.

## Cascading Threads of Story

The tales spun from a giant's loom,
Are stitched together with a big boom.
A yarn of joy in every twist,
Sometimes tangled, never missed!

Flying fish wear party hats,
As zebras dance with cute little cats.
Every story comes with a wink,
And all the clouds love to drink.

## Nature's Cloudy Embroidery

In the sky, a quilt unfurls,
With stitches made of giggling swirls.
Hiccups from the sunlight play,
While clouds call out, “Hey, ho, hooray!”

Monkeys on a trampoline,
Beneath the clouds, a lively scene.
Every breeze tells an old joke,
While teddy bears dance 'round the oak.

## Fabricated Fantasies Above

Fluffy pillows float on high,
A cat’s parade in the bright-sky.
Socks on clouds, a quirky sight,
Bananas dancing in pure delight.

Rainbows peek through cotton tan,
A fridge that flies, oh what a plan!
Chasing giggles in the breeze,
Pasta vines among the trees.

## Clouds Draped in Dreams

Jelly beans in fluffy space,
Cupcakes with a twinkly grace.
Marshmallow puffs that tickle noses,
Ticklish winds, the laughter poses.

Gummy bears bounce off the swirls,
Dizzying spins in cotton pearls.
A porcupine in bowtie flair,
Whispers secrets on a dare.

## Woven Wonders of the Ether

Twinkling stars with googly eyes,
Juggling fish beneath the skies.
A blanket stitched from giggly threads,
Worms that dance on tiny beds.

Flying toasters toast the sun,
Penguins racing for some fun.
Socks with legs and shoes for tails,
Off they dash on fluffy trails.

## A Diaphanous Journey Through Azure

Winds that carry cereal sails,
The sun winks and softly exhales.
Giggles echo in the blue,
Every cloud a laugh or two.

Cereal bars play hide and seek,
Waffle-trees begin to speak.
Splashing puddles, boots in flight,
In cloud-land, everything's just right.

**Abandoned Threads of the Day**

The sun trips on its final thread,
While shadows giggle, dance instead.
Each hour, a stitch left undone,
The day's a joke, oh what fun!

Whispers of twilight laugh and play,
As colors bleed and fade away.
A patchwork sky, a silly sight,
Even the stars are feeling light.

## Tearing Through the Silken Fabric

A squirrel skates on a silk cloud,
He dashes by, oh so loud!
Tails are tangled, flights a mess,
Who knew clouds could cause distress?

Feathers flutter, a comical scene,
A gentle breeze joins the routine.
With stitches frayed, they twist and twirl,
Nature's jesters do a whirl.

## Celestial Horizons in Harmony

The moon's a joker, winks and grins,
While stars play tag, seeing who wins.
Horizons giggle, the sky's a show,
A tapestry where dreams can flow.

Meteors swoosh with silly flair,
While comets sport a vaudeville air.
Galaxies spin, a cosmic dance,
In every twinkle, a playful glance.

## The Breath of Clouds Unfurled

A cloud took a sneeze, oh dear me,
Raindrops fell like jellybeans, whee!
Puffs of laughter filled the skies,
With every giggle, rainbows rise.

The winds are jesters, whistling tunes,
Playing tag with the cheeky boons.
Every breath a light-hearted jest,
In this charade, we’re truly blessed.

## Whispered Secrets of the Sky

When clouds puff up like marshmallow treats,
The sun winks down, teasing with beats.
Raindrops giggle, splashing with glee,
As birds wear hats, singing 'Look at me!'

Silly shapes dance in the blue,
A dinosaur sneezes—much ado.
Stars play hide and seek at night,
While the moon hums tunes, oh so light.

## Fabric of Twilight Dreams

In twilight's hush, wishes collide,
Where owls wear glasses, full of pride.
The stars knit stories with twinkling thread,
Tickling the dreams that float overhead.

Mice in tuxedos spin carousel,
Trading sweet cheese for a bright spell.
The sun yawns wide, teasing the moon,
While crickets play a merry tune.

## Embers of Light Amongst Shadows

Flickering candles play peekaboo,
Casting shadows that dance on cue.
A cheeky cat teases the night,
Wearing a bow tie, what a sight!

Fireflies twirl, lighting up the air,
While rabbits gossip without a care.
As the darkness craves some fun,
Even the bats join, on the run!

## Celestial Patterns in Motion

Stars do the cha-cha in the sky,
While comets wink as they whizz by.
The sun plays fetch with a fluffy cloud,
While rainbows giggle, looking proud.

Planets spin like tops in a race,
With alien dancers keeping pace.
Galaxies swirl in a cosmic spree,
Laughing at gravity, wild and free.

## Echoes from the Celestial Veil

In the sky, a giant sock,
Floating by, it takes a walk.
Clouds giggle, tickling the air,
Wondering how it got up there.

Stars are winking, all in jest,
While the moon is dressed the best.
A comet slips, dressed in green,
What a sight, it's quite the scene!

Raindrops dance on rooftops high,
Like little feet that jump and fly.
Each splash is laughter in disguise,
As puddles form with silly sighs.

The sun peeks out, a cheeky grin,
Saying, "Looks like we'll begin!"
With every twirl and silly spin,
It's playtime with a cosmic win!

## Beneath the Soft Tapestry

Balloons float in cotton candy skies,
Winking at birds who blink their eyes.
A squirrel in shades, taking a seat,
Cracks jokes with the ants at his feet.

Fluffy pillows drift, they make a nest,
While thunder giggles, feeling blessed.
The wind tells tales of lost socks,
As laughter echoes ‘round the blocks.

Clouds form shapes: a cat, a pie,
While raindrops dance, oh my, oh my!
With every puff, a chuckle grows,
As sunshine winks through twisty rows.

Whimsical whispers stir the breeze,
Tickling flowers, teasing the trees.
In the theater of air, we unite,
Where starlit giggles sparkle at night!

## A Dance of Ethereal Hues

Colors swirl in a playful spree,
Where orange polka-dots dance with glee.
Purple elephants on bicycles ride,
Round the laughter where giggles hide.

A rainbow sneezes, colors scatter,
Jumping jacks in the sky, what's the matter?
With pops of joy in every shade,
The clouds join in, no plans delayed.

Cloud yogurt spills on the green below,
While butterflies sing in a silly show.
Each drop's a smile, each wiggle a cheer,
As the sky laughs loud enough to hear!

Ethereal winks from the bright blue sea,
Tickling hearts, wild and free.
As dance-offs wage in soft light hues,
The spirit of fun is the day's best muse!

## Veils of Serenity Unraveled

A gown of mist, it flutters wide,
Like a proud bird on a joyful ride.
Whispers of breezes, gentle pranks,
As clouds form lines in playful ranks.

A rabbit hops on a moonbeam's path,
While rainbows giggle in a light-hearted math.
The sun throws a pie, what a mess!
As the stars lift up their sparkling dress.

Floating dreams on marshmallow waves,
With clouds that dance like surfboard braves.
Stars having tea with a fussy cat,
What a curious world, fancy that!

Veils slip, laughter fills the air,
As the sky plays dress-up with flair.
In this joyful, serene parade,
Every cloud’s a moment made!

## The Cloud's Gentle Undercurrent

Up in the sky, a fluff parade,
Cotton balls tumble, their colors invade.
A seagull looks up, gives a quizzical stare,
As rain droplet dancers do pirouettes in air.

Muffin-shaped clouds roll with laughter so bright,
Cackling at sunbeams that shine with delight.
A thunderstorm chuckles in boisterous tones,
While lightning juggles with sparkling stones.

## Floating Threads of Reflection

In the sky's loom, a whimsy so bold,
Bright threads of sunshine woven with gold.
Giggling shadows play peek-a-boo too,
As frolicsome breezes get tangled in blue.

Jellybean raindrops bounce off the ground,
A rainbow's giggle, hilariously found.
The sun plays a trick, a smile on its face,
Like a cheeky child, it lights up the place.

**Patterns Beneath the Whispering Canopy**

Beneath the canopy, whispers are sweet,
With squirrels hosting picnics, such a treat!
Chirping birds gossip in giggling spree,
While dandelions dance, a wild jubilee.

Breezes flirt lightly with leaves all around,
Tickling the branches, a soft, saucy sound.
A squirrel tightrope walks, balancing glee,
In a circus of wonders, they all feel so free.

## Celestial Weavings of Wonder

Stars twinkle mischief in a velvet gown,
Winking at night, smirking at frowns.
Cosmic threads spin tales in this wide embrace,
As comets throw parties, leading the race.

Planets play tag, with rings made of ice,
While meteors laugh, oh, ain't life so nice?
With sounds of the cosmos in twinkly array,
The universe grins, come join the ballet!

## The Gentle Tapestry of Twilight

Twilight tiptoes with a grin,
Painting the sky where dreams begin.
Cats wear hats, squirrels lounge with flair,
A jester moon shines, with a smile to spare.

Balloons float by on a fairy's whim,
Laughter unfolds in a twilight hymn.
Stars giggle softly, flickering bright,
As shadows play tricks in the fading light.

## Stitching Together Day and Night

Day at the door, all dressed in gold,
Night sneaks in, feeling quite bold.
They patch and sew with threads of delight,
Creating a quilt that hugs the night.

Sun hats and moon shoes, a curious sight,
A twinkle from Venus gives quite a fright.
Join hands, dear friends, in this fabric dance,
Where daytime grogginess won't take a chance.

## Glimmers of Color and Light

Colors collide in a wild balloon,
Waves of giggles rising to the moon.
Red apples jog, blueberries twirl,
In this tasty world, we all give a whirl.

Rainbows slip down like candy on strings,
Butterflies wear tuxedos, oh what kings!
Puppies in tuxes, prancing in glee,
This kaleidoscope giggle is wild and free.

## Dance of Illusions Amongst the Clouds

Clouds are dancers in a fluffy parade,
Juggling sunshine, never afraid.
They bounce and swirl, and tickle the sky,
As elephants fly and dandelions sigh.

In this whirlpool of whimsical flight,
Worms wear bowties, what a delight!
Each turn reveals a new song to hum,
As rainbows applaud, the cosmos goes numb.

## The Fabric of Transience

In the sky, a quilt of fluff,
Dancing puffs, a silly bluffs.
A cat might jump, a dog might bark,
Chasing clouds till it gets dark.

When the wind plays peek-a-boo,
You'd swear it knows just what to do.
Frolicking high, they twist and twirl,
Like a puppy in a perfect whirl.

Socks that lost their mates are here,
Waving goodbye, shedding a tear.
Cotton candy dreams accrue,
While squirrels in capes make their debut.

Fleeting, fleeting, paired in flight,
Every whim shines just so bright.
But catch them quick, or they will go,
Like your last slice of pizza, oh no!

## A Symphony of Airborne Patterns

Oh look! A parade of puffy fluff,
Music plays, but it’s kind of tough.
A tuba here, a trumpet there,
While kite strings tango in midair.

Balloons collide in a giggly mess,
Who knew wind could cause such stress?
Twists and turns, they throw a show,
Like a Broadway play for clouds! Bravo!

Pigeons wink, they're in on the joke,
Taking bets on who will choke.
A breeze that snickers, swirls with cheer,
While birds gossip, sipping cold beer.

With every breeze, the patterns shift,
A circus act, oh what a gift!
So lean back, let the laughter rise,
While marshmallow shapes dance in the skies!

## Whispers of Gossamer Dreams

Floating high, dreams gone astray,
Gossamer thoughts, don't run away!
Clouds play hide and seek for fun,
Kites that act like they weigh a ton.

A whisper here, a chuckle there,
As marshmallows spin without a care.
Joking jester, that soft gray fluff,
Tickling the sun—oh that’s enough!

Hats in the wind, what a sight!
Dancing like they’re in a fight.
Laugh out loud, don’t be a grump,
Every soar's a cheerful thump.

Pillow clouds with giggles stored,
Juggling starlight, never bored.
Join the frolic, spread your cheer,
As whimsical dreams hijack the sphere!

## Silhouettes of Skyward Threads

In the blue, threads of laughter play,
Tangled yarns from yesterday.
A sock fights back with a wink and grin,
As reality dips into a spin.

A moonlit joke, a starry snort,
Knitting joy in every sort.
Clouds that giggle, rain that drizzles,
As shadows dance and bubble fizzles.

The sun's bright smile, a cheeky tease,
While breezy breeches snag the trees.
Silhouettes weave and twirl and trot,
In this sky, we laugh a lot!

So join the stitching, thread the air,
A tapestry of joy laid bare.
Let silliness take you as it may,
In this patchwork, let’s come to play!

## Whispers of Woven Dreams

In the sky, a blanket lies,
Tickled by the sun's surprise.
Clouds are stitching, oh so tight,
A comfy quilt for day and night.

Rain drops bouncing, like a dance,
Puddles form, give frogs a chance.
The sunshine giggles, climbs up high,
Who knew clouds could wear a tie?

Cotton candy, drifting free,
Sweet, soft laughter, don’t you see?
Breezes tickle, flutter fast,
Woven whispers, how they last.

But watch your head, a bird may drop,
A feathered hat, a plopping flop.
With every chuckle, every sigh,
Dreams are stitched into the sky.

## Shadows in Silk

Underneath the fabric glow,
Shadows play, and winks they throw.
Silken threads begin to sway,
As sunbeams weave their clever play.

A dapper owl dons a shiny cloak,
Winks at frogs, a nifty joke.
Chasing shadows, wild and free,
Making mischief, just wait and see.

Breezy whispers float around,
Every puffy shape profound.
A bunny hops on cloud's fine seam,
Riding high on laughter's beam.

Down below, the folks all cheer,
As clouds parade, “What’s your fear?”
In this theater of soft delight,
Everyone is filled with light.

## Tapestry of Twilight

As twilight weaves a quirky tale,
Colors swirl like sails on gale.
Stars peek out in knit and purl,
A tapestry begins to twirl.

A dragonfly spins silk on cue,
Dressed in shadows, slightly askew.
Fireflies flicker, ready to play,
In this annual grand ballet.

Kites and giggles fill the air,
Chasing dreams without a care.
With each stitch, a dance is made,
In threads of night, a jester played.

So grab a star, and take a leap,
This fun-filled night will never sleep.
Laughter echoes, soft and bright,
In the fabric of the night.

## Threads of Heaven's Veil

Clouds are giggling, such a tease,
Woven patterns drift in breeze.
A curtain of dreams, soft and light,
Hide and seek with the moon tonight.

Silly shapes take flight with glee,
A cat is dancing up a tree!
A moose in boots goes for a stroll,
While clouds above begin to roll.

Each breeze whispers a tiny jest,
The sun just chuckles, never rests.
A patchwork quilt of funny sights,
Turns every moment into flights.

So join the laughter, don't delay,
In this whimsical, sky-bound play.
With every thread, a story told,
A tapestry of fun unfolds.

## Journeys Across Layers of Air

In cozy puffs they journey, bright,
Balloons with dreams take wing in flight.
They bob and weave, a wobbly make,
As munching clouds giggle, for fun's sake.

A seagull swoops, a sneaky tease,
Whispers, "Birdies, dance with ease!"
Over fields where funny frogs jump,
While squirrels practice their best trumpet jump.

We ride on waves of fluff and cheer,
With sandwiches packed, oh dear, oh dear!
Each bite a bounce, how we all sway,
Belly laughs help chase clouds away.

So up we go, with a glimmering grin,
Past cotton candy lands that spin.
Adventures swirl in the sky's embrace,
With laughter echoing through the space.

## A Tapestry in the Gentle Winds

A woven tale of giggles bright,
Where zephyrs dance, and spirits ignite.
Socks on trees, a playful sight,
Fluffy whispers tease in the sunlight.

Kites tumble down, an unplanned fall,
Colorful chaos, a laughter call.
With every breeze, a joke unfolds,
As the laughing moon in its splendor scolds.

Boats made of leaves drift on a stream,
They sail with whimsy, dream by dream.
The frogs make jokes in croaks so sweet,
While butterflies bob to a bouncy beat.

We stitch our tales with sunshine beams,
In skies of whimsy, laughter gleams.
With threads of joy through breezes we wind,
In this funny lace, true fun we find.

## The Whispering Plains of Wonder

Upon the grass where whispers dwell,
Funny breezes break the spell.
Each ticklish thought takes flight so high,
Fluffy daisies giggle as they sigh.

The clouds wear hats, a curious style,
Like fluffy gnomes, they grin and smile.
They trade their jokes, a cloudy swap,
While silly shadows bounce and hop.

A stampede of ants in a line so neat,
Doing a dance, oh what a feat!
They scurry and dash with a wink and a nod,
Creating a scene that surely would prod.

On endless plains where giggles bloom,
The echoing laughter disperses gloom.
With every breeze, a spell we weave,
In whispers of wonder, we all believe.

## Ethereal Patterns Above Us

In skies of cotton, silly shapes play,
A snail's slow slide—why not today?
They puff and tumble, oh what a sight,
As they tease the sun with pure delight.

A chaotic dance of bright balloons,
Spinning laughter in chubby dunes.
With every gust, they play a tune,
As if tickled by the chubby moon.

Silly geese in a unison flight,
Making faces, oh what a sight!
They wobble and weave in feathery glee,
As if practice for a comedy spree.

Across the canvas of our hearts,
A painted laughter, where joy imparts.
In patterns ethereal, light and free,
We cherish the fun, just you and me.

## Hidden Crafted Whispers

In the attic, a sock's on the run,
Hiding from pairs, it’s just no fun.
Whispers of fabric, a silkiness neat,
Dancing in corners where dust bunnies meet.

Buttons are laughing with threads so tight,
Arguing gently about who's more right.
A spool of mischief, with needle's slight wink,
Crafting a tale that makes all hearts sink.

A cloak made of giggles, it’s perfect for play,
Worn by the cat who just won’t obey.
Fashioned from fluff, with a twist and a twirl,
Creating a chaos, oh what a swirl!

Under the bed, a sock puppet prances,
Telling stories of lost second chances.
With every stitch, an adventure begins,
In the fabric of jest, where laughter always wins.

## Echoes in the Wind's Fabric

A kite with a tail made of laughter so bright,
Soaring through skies, in a whimsical flight.
Its ribbons are tickles, a breeze just can't hold,
Whispering secrets of mischief untold.

A squirrel in socks miscalculates jumps,
Landing in bushes, with all of his thumps.
Nutty as ever, he giggles away,
Telling the sun that it’s time to play.

Clouds like cotton, drifting so slow,
Caught in a riddle, just putting on shows.
They tickle the rooftops, whisper old rhymes,
While rainbows are chuckling, jiving in chimes.

In this tapestry woven of silly delight,
Every corner hums with joy, day or night.
The wind plays a tune that makes children dance,
Crafting their giggles, giving dreams a chance.

## Silken Fragments of a Dream

Clouds draped like velvet, a whimsical sight,
Sometimes they frolic and dance in the light.
A button-eyed owl gives a wink from above,
While stars throw confetti, like giggles of love.

A pocket of fluff with pebbles so round,
Sings lullabies softly where wishes are found.
Doodles of daylight swirl on a whim,
Crafting odd forms that make night slightly dim.

Dreams tangled like yarn, in a twist and a curl,
Where laughter escapes and the wildness can swirl.
Ticklish sensations from dusk fill the air,
As night wears a grin, with naught a single care.

In the silken fragments, we find little glee,
As giggles bounce high, wild, and free.
Leave fear at the door, let the silliness stream,
For every odd moment is part of the dream.

## Artistry of Atmospheric Hues

Colors of whimsy paint skies in a jest,
Pink and blue giggles, the sun's playful vest.
Each hue a chuckle, each shade a sweet grin,
A rainbow retreats with a nod and a spin.

Puffy floaters parade in a playful ballet,
Where clouds tiptoe softly, mischievously sway.
An artist in puffs, dreams draped in embrace,
Tickling the twilight with a fun-loving grace.

Stars giggle quietly, twinkling on cue,
Each one a punchline in a cosmic view.
In the gallery sky, laughter hangs low,
Framing the moon in its silvery glow.

Whimsical sunsets become crafty scenes,
Capturing moments like childhood's soft dreams.
Each brush of the wind sings of joy and surprise,
In this artistry drawn from the wild, laughing skies.

## A Dance of Fabric in Flight

Up in the sky, the napkins twirled,
Dancing in breezes, with laughter unfurled.
Bouncing like children on swings in the sun,
Who knew a tablecloth could have so much fun?

They jumped over rooftops, they soared with delight,
Only to land in a giant dog's bite!
The fabric just giggled, with threads that gleamed,
Those playful mishaps? Oh, they simply dreamed!

## Fables Stitched with Sunlight

A quilt woven tales of a cat on a spree,
Chasing the shadows of birds, you see.
Each stitch a memory, passed down with a wink,
Who knew a patch could be so prone to stink?

Under the sun's watchful smile so wide,
The threads shared secrets, they simply can't hide.
A story of socks that went off to roam,
One flew to space while the others found home!

## Weightless Patterns in the Blue

Balloons in the air, dressed up like a show,
Racing each other with nowhere to go.
They giggled and twisted, like clouds on the run,
Dreaming of marshmallows all warm and yum!

Patterns in chaos, a kaleidoscope spree,
Spinning and swirling, oh, what glee!
Who knew a fabric could tickle the sky?
While wrappers of candy flirted nearby!

## The Seamstress of the Horizon

There’s a seamstress weaving with threads made of light,
Stitching up sunsets that sparkle at night.
With a needle of giggles and fabric of dreams,
She crafts silly hats with oversized seams.

Her laughter, infectious, her patterns askew,
Each cloud a creation, a whimsical view.
A jester in sky, she replaces the gray,
With ribbons of joy and a dainty bouquet!

## Celestial Embroidery in Flight

Up in the sky, a strange sight,
Birds wearing hats, oh what a flight!
They twirl and spin with grace so grand,
And dance like they've a master plan.

Each cloud a cushion, soft and white,
They dive and swoop, what pure delight!
An owl wears glasses, a true oddball,
Who knew the skies could hold a ball?

## Stitches of Light and Shadow

A squirrel on a cloud, quite absurd,
Knitting rainbows, what a word!
He drops a stitch, the sun does peek,
Now everyone is playing hide and seek.

With threads of dusk and dawn intertwined,
The moon chuckles at the mismatched kind.
Stars are buttons sewn up tight,
A cosmic quilt, what a sight!

## Chasing the Shimmering Breeze

A ladybug chased a flickering ray,
In a game of tag, they'd frolic and play.
Grasshoppers joining in the spree,
While butterflies sip on tea for free.

Fluffy shapes parade like little clowns,
Wearing mustaches, laughing sounds.
The breeze joins in with a ticklish tease,
As everyone dances with playful ease.

## Clouds Adorned with Delicate Traces

Clouds with sweatbands, jogging so fast,
Huffing and puffing, what a blast!
They flaunt their styles, oh such flair,
While puffballs gossip, without a care.

A breeze that tickles, a cheerful tune,
Spreading giggles 'neath the moon.
With each fluff there’s a spark of fun,
Creating mischief 'til day is done.

## A Tapestry of Misty Reflections

Giggles weave through the skies,
Like whispers of playful sighs.
Clouds wear their coats of white fluff,
While rain tries to hide its tough stuff.

Sun spills juice on the day,
While shadows dance out to play.
A ticklish breeze gives a shove,
And the sky laughs with playful love.

Puffy shapes in silly poses,
Look closely, they're quite the roses.
A bear and a cat in a race,
Who knew clouds had such a face?

With dreamy colors all around,
In this jest, joy is found.
So let's twirl with the puffed-up fun,
Until we all melt into one.

## Dreaming in Soft Spun Hues

In a world of cotton candy skies,
Where laughter races and seldom lies.
Each hue spins a tale of delight,
As we chase the frolic through the night.

Fluffy shapes try on silly hats,
A parade of clouds and cheery chats.
One thinks he's a wise old owl,
While another struts with a pretend scowl.

Giggling stars join the throng,
Whispers of moonlight drift along.
With wild dreams in soft spun thread,
We pillow fight with clouds overhead.

So let's giggle until we ache,
In the land where the silly clouds wake.
For in this canvas of light and cheer,
Every breath fills with laughter here.

## The Sky's Gentle Embrace

Balloons float in the bright blue sea,
Dancing in air, wild and free.
Ticklish breezes hug the day,
While sunshine giggles and leans to play.

Gentle whispers hide in the folds,
Where colors shimmer like dreams retold.
Clouds hide jokes up their fluffy sleeves,
As shadows sneak out like mischief thieves.

Every wink from the morning's glow,
Turns the air into a show.
While rain showers sprinkle with glee,
It's a slapstick sketch in a sky jubilee.

As we drift in this laughter sleep,
With joy to catch and dreams to keep.
The sky's embrace, so soft and sweet,
Wraps us in its artistic feat.

## Hues of Illusion and Wonder

The horizon giggles in bright hues,
While playful whispers blow like a fuse.
Clouds morph into creatures that prance,
A dragon that dances, a pig's silly glance.

Sunlight nudges the shadows awake,
Tickling dreams in the paths that we make.
Colors jump in a dizzy array,
Mistakes become art in a comical display.

With every glance, a fresh surprise,
A kite caught in a web of blue skies.
As clouds play dress-up in dazzling shades,
Life's woven humor never fades.

So lift your eyes towards the sky,
Join in the laughter, don't be shy.
With each twist of fate's gentle hand,
We'll paint the world, goofy and grand.

## Clouds in a Tidal Embrace

A fluffy wave rolls in with glee,
Kites dance above, wild and free.
With a pinch of rain, they giggle aloud,
Splashing joy on the unsuspecting crowd.

In a wind-swept toss, they twist and twine,
Sunbeams wink as stars realign.
Tidal breezes take their cue,
And pull a prank or two, just for you.

## Netting the Sky's Secrets

A fishing net stretched wide and far,
To catch the whispers of a passing star.
But all it caught was a sock and a shoe,
And the clouds cheekily giggled, 'What of you?'

They tangled their thoughts with knots and jests,
While daydreams floated in fancy vests.
To weave the tales of skies so vast,
Where silly thoughts drift and dance at last.

## Soft Embrace of Afternoon

Bubbling laughter in warm sunlight,
Clouds play hide-and-seek, oh what a sight!
Pillows of fluff, drifting high and wide,
They peek and poke, giggling inside.

Within their fluff, soft secrets dwell,
Like a tickle fight, all's well and swell.
Rustling leaves in a teasing tone,
“Catch us if you can, you're on your own!”

## Interwoven with the Wind

The wind whispers jokes, oh so sly,
As clouds weave tales that tickle the sky.
One cloud trips, in a tumble so grand,
And all from above burst into laughter, unplanned.

They braid their blunders with playful grace,
Creating a dance, a light-hearted race.
With breezy giggles, they spin around,
Chasing the sunlight, spreading joy abound.

## Starlit Patterns Above

Up in the night, a dance unfolds,
Stars playing peek-a-boo, so bold.
They giggle and twirl, in cosmic cheer,
Who knew celestial orbs could jeer?

With winks and smiles, they stitch the sky,
A pattern of mischief, oh so spry.
Planets bounce in a wobbly line,
Creating a quilt, oh isn’t it fine?

A comet trips, what a silly sight!
As it sends a shooting star to flight.
The constellations swap a silly joke,
And in their laughter, the darkness broke.

So raise a glass to the twinkly crew,
Who weave the night with laughter anew.
For every star that winks and glows,
Leaves us smiling as the night wind blows.

## Breath of the Infinite Veil

Whispers float on the breeze today,
A veil that flutters, come what may.
It tickles the cheeks, a gentle tease,
As if the air has got a slight sneeze.

Each puff a giggle, echoing free,
Carrying jokes from the boughs of a tree.
Leaves chuckle softly, rustling bright,
Talking about the mix-ups of flight.

Clouds shape-shift with a playful grin,
Doubling as hippos and then a tin.
They play make-believe with pompous flair,
Hiding the sun, oh they just don't care!

So take a breath and join the fun,
In this tapestry spun beneath the sun.
For laughter is woven with each gust,
Creating a quilt of joy and trust.

## The Softness of Day’s Embrace

Morning yawns and stretches wide,
As pillows fluff and sunlight glide.
The day tiptoes, soft as a cat,
Whispering secrets, imagine that!

A coffee cup's laughter fills the air,
With every sip, a light-hearted dare.
The toast pops up, spring-loaded cheer,
“Catch me!” it shouts, with nippy sneer.

Socks collide in a colorful war,
Mismatched soldiers, oh the uproar!
They dance in pairs with great delight,
Waging a battle from morning till night.

As the sun grins down, spreading joy,
Every shadow plays, a light-hearted ploy.
In this embrace, we find a space,
Where laughter and love interlace.

## Floating Threads of Imagination

In the sky, thoughts drift and sail,
Each one a story, a whimsy trail.
With giggly gigabytes twinkling bright,
They chase the clouds, a playful flight.

Ideas tumble like a clumsy cat,
Knocking over dreams, imagine that!
As they stitch together a curious plot,
Creating a tapestry of what is, and what's not.

Each thread a whisper, a fabled chance,
Inviting the world to join the dance.
With spirals of laughter, they intertwine,
Filling the void with silly design.

So let your thoughts float, twirl and spin,
In this grand workshop, let the fun begin!
For every thread that stretches and bends,
Brings us closer, where laughter transcends.

## Secrets Woven in the Wind

Whispers tumble through the air,
Like socks that vanish everywhere.
When breezes howl and giggles fly,
You might just catch a chicken's sigh.

The leaves are dancing, what a sight!
A squirrel joins to steal the night.
Each gust brings tales that seem absurd,
Of clouds that gossip, quite unheard.

A dragon sneezes, what a flare,
It sends a kite high in the square.
With every puff, a secret spins,
Of playful clouds with foolish grins.

So let the whispers swirl and twirl,
As nature laughs and colors swirl.
For in the breeze, the jesters meet,
In fluffy coats and breeze-kissed feet.

## Each Cloud a Silent Story

Oh look, a cloud with a fuzzy hat,
It drifts along, can you believe that?
With every puffy breath it takes,
It shares the news of silly wakes.

A duck named Fred floats by with flair,
We all just stare, it doesn't care.
It quacks a joke, we roll with glee,
While cloud-cyclones spin around a tree.

The stories told in shades of white,
Of lonesome raindrops, taking flight.
A rambunctious breeze that tickles toes,
As we all wonder where the time goes.

So next time you look up and smile,
Know those clouds have danced a while.
They hold more laughs than you can see,
Each fluffy friend a mystery.

## Where Dreams Fray at the Edges

Up above where giggles sprout,
A patchwork sky has dreams without doubt.
But sometimes threads slip from their seams,
And float away on whimsy's beams.

My dreams are tangled like tangled hair,
They knot and twist in the warm air.
With every puff, they trip and fall,
Each one a riddle, each one a squall.

A seagull cackles at a wayward star,
It knows they're lost, but plays bizarre.
While I look up, my mind's in knots,
Creating stories from silly thoughts.

So if you spy those fraying dreams,
Just tug a string, or so it seems.
For every laugh that spins away,
Is just a ploy for a brighter day.

## Shades of Eternity Entwined

In colors bright, the sky does scheme,
Splashes of laughter in a painter's dream.
Each stroke a giggle, each hue a prank,
Where the sun winks, and the rivers thank.

As clouds parade in a funky line,
They twirl and sway, feeling divine.
A rainbow hiccups, what a sight,
Filling the sky with pure delight.

So gather 'round, let’s share a cheer,
For every shade a joke is near.
From violet blush to emerald tease,
Eternity’s laughter dances with ease.

So let us bask in this funny light,
Where colors twist and dreams ignite.
For every moment skyward bound,
Is more than beauty; it’s joy profound.

## Weaving Whispers in the Air

In the sky a joke unfurls,
With giggles caught on twirls.
Birds are knitting with a grin,
Sewing laughter from within.

Clouds tease the sun and moon,
Like children in a merry tune.
They trade secrets, float and dive,
Tickling breezes, feel alive!

A squirrel wears a puffy hat,
While bees buzz round like chitchat.
Each puff has something to say,
A wink, a laugh, they drift away.

So if you gaze up to the skies,
Catch a giggle, hold the prize.
In the fabric up so high,
Whispers weave as clouds go by.

## Beneath the Feathery Veil

Underneath the fluffy fluff,
It's a world just a bit tough.
Clouds play peekaboo with glee,
While raindrops dance like they're free.

Jokes are hidden in the breeze,
Tangled up in budding trees.
The sun shines bright, oh what a treat,
As puddles giggle at our feet!

A rabbit hops by with a frown,
Spilling drops of golden brown.
It's coffee from the sky above,
Pouring laughter, mix of love.

In the waltz of air we find,
Funny whispers, tickled mind.
Underneath the quilted hue,
Life's a jest, and so are you!

## Threads of Hope in the Atmosphere

Hopes are stitched with silver thread,
Float around like dreams in bed.
They twirl around the bluest heights,
As laughter blooms in clouded sights.

A dandelion takes a ride,
With giggles bouncing side to side.
The horizon wears a silly grin,
While dreams chase clouds, oh where to begin?

Kites make friends with every breeze,
Winking at the playful trees.
Each gust gives a silly shout,
As if to say, there's no doubt!

Peeking out from misty seams,
Are playful jests and funny dreams.
In the vastness where we tread,
Threads of mirth will guide our heads.

## Glistening Strings of Daydreams

Daydreams dangle on a line,
Sparkling like an old wine sign.
Clouds parade in poofy shoes,
While the sun winks with good news.

A bouncing frog joins in the spree,
Telling tales with utmost glee.
Rainbow tails up in the sky,
Twisting like a pie gone by.

Stars giggle, peek and play,
As they sketch the night away.
Each glimmer wraps a tale divine,
In the atmosphere where dreams align.

So, look above, take in the laugh,
Every cloud, a playful daft.
In this theater so grand and bright,
Strings of joy dance into the night.

## The Soft Breath of Dreamscape

In a realm where giggles float,
Pandas wear hats and do the most.
A fish on a bike sings out loud,
Tickling the fancy of every cloud.

Fluffy sheep jump over my bed,
Counting me instead of dread.
The moon wears glasses, quite absurd,
Whispers of laughter, all heard.

Bubbles of laughter fill the air,
While cats perform in underwear.
Chasing their tails, quite the sight,
Creating a ruckus every night.

So dance with shadows, let them gleam,
Silly dreams are but a scheme.
In this land where joy free falls,
Life's a joke, and laughter calls.

## Fragments of Light on a Canvas Sky

Stars wear sneakers, just for fun,
They prance around until they run.
A sunbeam giggles, tickles the sea,
While surfboards dance with glee.

Clouds on stilts walk in a line,
At a carnival, sipping fine wine.
Raindrops play chess with leaves in the park,
Meeting up clearly after dark.

Kites have conversations in the breeze,
Stealing ice cream from bumblebees.
They argue about colors, red and blue,
With the sun as their referee too.

So, twirl in the sparkles of bright delight,
In this wacky show from day to night.
Every moment's a playful spree,
Fragments of joy, wild and free.

## Amongst the Interlaced Whispers

Socks and sandals dance on twirls,
As giggles play with twinkling pearls.
A bird in a tux, what a delight,
Singing to stars in the dead of night.

Chickens debate the best kind of shoes,
While mice spin tales of whimsical blues.
Their laughter weaves through the tangled vines,
Creating magic in playful lines.

Butterflies play hopscotch on rain,
Spreading cheer, easing the pain.
Whiskers twitch as cats spin tall tales,
Of daring escapades and fishy trails.

Among the whispers, fun does lie,
In this cosmos where dreams fly high.
So join the chatter, be a part,
Of this joyous jesting, a work of art.

## Whispered Threads of Tomorrow

Kites are busy sipping on tea,
Chatting about what they could be.
A squirrel juggles acorns, quite proud,
While a cheeky raccoon cheers loud.

Jellybeans rain from cotton candy skies,
As giggles explode in colorful ties.
Tooth fairies crash at parties galore,
Trading sweets for dreams—and more!

Whiskers and wings, they play tag,
Bouncing through clouds in a colorful rag.
Fish in bow ties swim with grace,
Chasing gold stars in a sparkling race.

Embrace the silliness life brings,
In tomorrow's thread where laughter sings.
A tapestry woven with joy and cheer,
In this world of fun, let's persevere.

## A Symphony of Floating Fabrics

A quilt of white, so high and bright,
Flutters and dances, what a sight!
Socks do the tango, shirts take a chance,
While breezes twirl them in a romancing stance.

Naps are interrupted by cotton ballet,
An umbrella joins in, oh what a fray!
Patchwork flirts with mismatched shoes,
As raindrops giggle, chasing the blues.

Pillow fights are whispered in the air,
In a caper of textiles, no time to spare!
Each fabric flying, the sky's a show,
Yarn won't be still, it longs to flow.

With every gust, a fabric spree,
Laughing threads, as happy can be.
In this charade, the world plays along,
Who knew that fabrics could dance so strong!

## Celestial Weavings of Hope

Look up and see the cottony crew,
Stitching up dreams in a sky so blue.
Buttons twinkle, threads start to chirp,
Clouds become cozy, like a wraparound burp!

Feathers are hanging, not just for looks,
As they whisper tales in crafty books.
A playful breeze with a sneaky twist,
Ties knots of laughter in a comic mist.

Puffs of fluff glide by with a laugh,
In this great tale, they're the paragraph!
With a wink and a giggle, they spread delight,
As the sun winks back with glorious light.

So raise a toast to this fabric display,
As we laugh with the clouds, frolicking away!
In the tapestry of life, there's a funny bend,
With threads of joy that never seem to end!

## Rainbow Threads from the Sky

A splash of color, a whimsy parade,
With ribbons of joy, the clouds are laid.
Stripes of laughter, and spots of cheer,
In this lively fest, nothing to fear!

Kites in the making, joined by a stew,
Of poppyseed puffs in a vibrant hue.
They wrestle and tumble, a sight to behold,
What a comedy show as the skies unfold!

Ticklish winds bring giggles galore,
While buttoned-up clouds continue to soar.
To the cheerful tune of a patchwork band,
Every blushing thread forms a playful hand.

So hold your breath, the sky's in a spin,
As laughter rings true beneath their skin!
With every sky stitch, the world feels bright,
In a thread of joy, let’s take flight!

## Threads of Reflection in the Air

Look at those threads, la-dee-da!
They're having a party, oh la la!
Mirrored giggles float on by,
As the fabrics waltz in the evening sky.

A patchwork of pratfalls, what a scene,
Tangled up t-shirts act like a queen.
Threads of humor, flutter with glee,
In this airy circus, wild and free!

Pants fly solo, socks in a pair,
Chasing the clouds without a care.
Dancing in circles, they join the fun,
As sunshine giggles, oh what a run!

With every twist, a story unfolds,
In the tapestry of joy that never gets old.
Through laughter and threads, we shall share,
The delight of life that's floating up there!

## A Drift of Hope in the Sky

A fluffy puff, it floats so high,
Like grandma's scarf, it catches the eye.
With a wink of sun, it sways in place,
Dancing round, like an old clown's grace.

Chasing shadows, tickling the trees,
Whispering jokes in the gentle breeze.
The world below, it watches and sighs,
As cotton candy drifts in playful skies.

A squishy form that brings a smile,
Like wedged-up socks, it's worth your while.
Its giggles echo, it's a funny sight,
Oh, what a show in pure delight!

So let it drift, let laughter soar,
In a land of dreams, who could want more?
With a twist and turn, it floats about,
Bringing joy and laughter, without a doubt.

## The Gentle Embrace of Fabric Above

Up high, a blanket with fluff and care,
Hides in laughter, sweet as a pear.
It gathers tight like a hug that's warm,
Wiggly and jiggly, creating a charm.

Like socks in a dryer, spinning around,
It makes the world giggle, a joyous sound.
Stretching wide, it can tickle too,
A soft, silly quilt, just for you.

Whipping and whooshing, it paints the sky,
With scribbles of joy, it’s a crafty lie.
A playful embrace that won't let you go,
Bringing giggles, like a comedy show.

So thank the fluff above your head,
For the silly joy it freely spreads.
It’s laughter's gift, wrapped up with pride,
In a world of whimsy, we all can glide.

## Patterns Unseen on the Wind

In breezy dances, secrets unfold,
Whirling around, like stories told.
Patterns so vivid, yet hard to see,
Like a dance of socks under the sea.

Tiptoeing whispers, they flit and fly,
Chasing the leaves as they wave goodbye.
The mischief plays upon the air,
Winked at by clouds with a haughty flair.

They flutter about with a cheeky grin,
Like sneaky socks that run to win.
Hiding in corners, they twirl and leap,
With laughter resonating, making hearts leap.

So watch for the fun in every breeze,
When patterns emerge that aim to please.
A silly jig from air's gentle hand,
Creating a ruckus across the land.

## A Journey Beyond the Veil

Beyond the fold, the mischief waits,
Plans some giggles, and funny debates.
With every fluff, a new plot springs,
As laughter echoes and joy it brings.

Floating away, with a twist and twirl,
Like a kite in chaos, giving a whirl.
It teases the sun, and plays with shade,
Crafting a riddle that won't soon fade.

Meandering lightly, a jest unfolds,
As yarn-like laughter just never molds.
Flowing freely, till the day is done,
Silly threads, weaving webs of fun.

So journey forth with your heart in hand,
Laughing with clouds, dancing in the sand.
For in this chase, joy is the goal,
As we twine and drift, we're rich in soul.

www.ingramcontent.com/pod-product-compliance
Lightning Source LLC
Chambersburg PA
CBHW051732290426
43661CB00122B/243
* 9 7 8 1 8 0 5 8 6 0 2 4 2 *